THE HIGH PROTEIN COOK
LOUISE KANG
100 **HIGH PROTEIN** BREAKFASTS

This book is dedicated to my son, Ale.

I would also like to thank Willy Wong, Kay Smith,
Samantha Mason, Colette Mason, AJ Silvers and Margaret Carr.

Published 2017 by Kang Media
Copyright © Louise Kang, 2017

Photographs on pages 26, 36, 40, 44 and 59 © William Wong
All other photographs © Louise Kang

Design & typesetting by Kay Smith at Agrada.

The right of Louise Kang to be identified as the author of this work has been
asserted by her in accordance with the Copyright, Designs and Patents Act 1988.

CONTENTS

100 HIGH PROTEIN BREAKFASTS

When it comes to a high protein diet, breakfast is *the* meal that many of us struggle with. Think about it: the typical western breakfast of sugary cereal or toast with lashings of butter and jam isn't exactly packed full of protein.

I've created *100 High Protein Breakfasts* to help you out. This book is packed full of high protein breakfast ideas and recipes – everything from 4-minute quickies to luxurious weekend treats.

This book is not a pretty coffee table book with glossy pictures of recipes you will never make. Instead, it's a practical straight-to-the-point ideas book. The recipes are simple, and this is intentional – I *want* you to build upon them, adapt them and give them your own twist.

I got so carried away with creating this book, I ended up with too many recipes – you can download the extras at highp.ro/breakfasts.

Let me know how you get on – if you post any pictures of your creations, please tag me in.

Louise

Louise

highproteincook.com
facebook.com/highproteincook
instagram.com/highproteincook

P.S. Gone are the days when you had to find a publisher, a food photographer and stylist before you could create a recipe book. Over half of the pictures in this book are from my Instagram (and taken in my kitchen with my iPhone). If you are interested in creating your own recipe book, head to louisekang.com/cookbook.

RECIPE NOTES

- *high protein yoghurt refers to any yoghurt with a protein content of around 11g per 100g (e.g. Greek yoghurt or skyr)*
- *all eggs are medium*
- *any kind of milk can be used (macros are based on unsweetened almond milk)*
- *any kind of sugar or sweetener can be used (macros are based on a low-calorie sweetener)*
- *all US imperial measurements are approximate – use the metric measurements for best results*
- *all macros are approximate and are intended as a guideline only*

OATS

Is there anything more comforting when it's cold outside than a warm bowl of oats? Plus, if you do any kind of endurance sports, oats are fantastic fuel.

Why choose oats?

Basically, they will keep you full for ages. This is because oats contain beta-glucans, a type of soluble fibre that slows down the absorption of carbs into the bloodstream. Or, in other words, they are considered low GI.

There are many ways to eat oats – turn the page for some ideas.

Are oats high in protein?

Not really – 100g of oats has 17g of protein compared to 66g of carbs. This means a single serving of 50g will have 8½ grams of protein.

BUT it's really easy to pair oats with thick dairy (i.e. Greek yoghurt) or protein shakes.

PROTEIN PORRIDGE

Porridge is the ultimate comfort food, popular since medieval times. There are many ways to customise porridge, so you will never get bored of it.

THE BASIC RECIPE

SERVES 1
5 MINS PREP
5 MINS COOK

INGREDIENTS
45g/½ cup porridge oats
250ml/1 cup milk
plus
  extra protein
  sugar/sweetener
  toppings

METHOD

1. Mix the oats and milk together. Heat gently on the hob or in the microwave for around 4 – 5 minutes.

2. Stir in the extra protein and transfer to a bowl.

3. Top with sugar/sweetener and toppings – see ideas overleaf.

THE EXTRA PROTEIN
Bump up the protein with one of the following options:

- Protein powder dissolved in a little milk or water. If you are using a dairy-based protein powder such as whey or casein, be sure to add it right at the end so it doesn't curdle. Half a scoop has around 10g of extra protein.

- Thick dairy such as Greek yoghurt, skyr or quark. A heaped tablespoon has around 6g of extra protein.

- An egg white. This may seem like a strange idea, but it really works. You won't be able to taste it, but it thickens the porridge. 1 egg white has around 4g of extra protein.

- Whey crispies.[1] 1 scoop has around 5g of extra protein.

THE SUGAR/SWEETENER
Choose between a sugar such as maple syrup, agave or coconut sugar or a calorie-free sweetener.[1] 1 teaspoon of sugar has around 17 calories and 4g carbs - if you opt for sugar, don't forget to add these to the macros below.

THE TOPPINGS - see overleaf for ideas

> *If you spend any time on Instagram, you will have heard of 'zoats'. Grate some courgette into the porridge while the oats are cooking. You won't be able to taste it, but it adds bulk and also helps you to hit your 5-a-day. Double win!*

 195 CALORIES 6g PROTEIN 6g FAT 28g CARBS

MACROS (excluding protein, sweetener and toppings)

[1] *For details of where to find this, go to highproteincook.com/breakfast*

Greek yoghurt, brown sugar substitute, banana and pomegranate

PORRIDGE 8 WAYS

1. **CARROT CAKE PORRIDGE**
   Grate a **small carrot** and add it into the pan/microwave-safe bowl together with the oats and milk. Add **½ tsp ground ginger, a grating of nutmeg** and **10 raisins** together with your choice of protein and sweetener (I used Greek yoghurt and brown sugar substitute).

2. **SALTED CARAMEL PORRIDGE**
   Add **3 Medjool dates, ½ tsp salted caramel flavouring** and **3 tbsp warm water** into a small bowl. Leave to soak for around 15 minutes, until the dates are tender. Remove the stones from the dates and liquidise into a paste. Stir into the porridge, add some extra protein and top with walnuts.

3. Cottage cheese, banana, cherries, seeds and maple syrup

4. Vanilla whey protein powder, banana and walnuts

5. Egg white, berries, seeds and maple syrup

6. 'Zoats', Greek yoghurt, mango, seeds and zero-calorie syrup

7. Quark, strawberries, bananas and zero-calorie syrup

8. Skyr, brown sugar substitute, berries and whey protein crispies

1.

2.

PROTEIN GRANOLA

The big advantage of making your own granola is you control exactly what goes into it. This recipe has very little sugar – only a little maple syrup and apple juice to take the edge off the artificial sweeteners contained in the protein powder. Don't be tempted to leave out the cardamom seeds – they're the recipe's secret weapon.

SERVES 8
10 MINS PREP
20 MINS COOK

INGREDIENTS

160g/1½ cups porridge oats

100g/½ cup coconut oil

60ml/¼ cup maple syrup

4 tbsp apple juice

50g/½ cup/2 scoops vanilla whey protein powder

1 tsp ground cinnamon

150g/1 cup mixed nuts and seeds, roughly chopped

2 tbsp desiccated coconut

seeds of 8 cardamom pods

METHOD

1. Preheat oven to 180°C/350°F.

2. Spoon the coconut oil into the baking tray and put in the oven to melt while the oven is warming up. Once melted, pour the oil into a mixing bowl and leave to cool for around 5 minutes.

3. Add the maple syrup, apple juice, vanilla whey and cinnamon to the bowl and mix to form a paste.

4. Add the oats, nuts and seeds, desiccated coconut and cardamom seeds to the bowl and mix until everything is coated with the paste.

5. Pour this mixture into the baking tray and bake for at least 20 minutes, stirring a few times so the top layer doesn't burn. If you want the granola to be extra crispy, bake for a little longer.

6. Once done to your liking, remove tray from the oven and serve.

> ### RECIPE NOTES
>
> - *This recipe is completely customisable: replace the vanilla whey with any kind of flavoured protein powder – plant or dairy – and add your favourite nuts, seeds and dried fruit. Or, if you want to cut the calories, leave the nuts out, replace the maple syrup with a zero-calorie syrup and use water rather than apple juice.*
>
> - *Nuts burn easily, so keep the tray away from the top of your oven and don't forget to stir the mixture a few times. Alternatively, you can add the nuts towards the end of the cooking time.*

340 CALORIES **11g** PROTEIN **23g** FAT **21g** CARBS

MACROS (per serving, granola only)

GOJI GRANOLA BALLS

These protein-packed balls are so versatile – instead of goji berries you could add raisins, coconut shavings, nuts or even chocolate chips.

MAKES 6 BALLS
5 MINS PREP

INGREDIENTS

30g/¼ cup/1 scoop porridge oats

25g/¼ cup/1 scoop vanilla whey protein powder

1 tbsp honey

2 tbsp almond butter

2 tbsp milk

10g goji berries

METHOD

Mix all of the ingredients together, adding more milk if too dry or more oats or protein powder if too wet. Shape into 6 balls and keep chilled until it's time to eat.

 80 CALORIES **5g** PROTEIN **4g** FAT **7g** CARBS

MACROS (per ball)

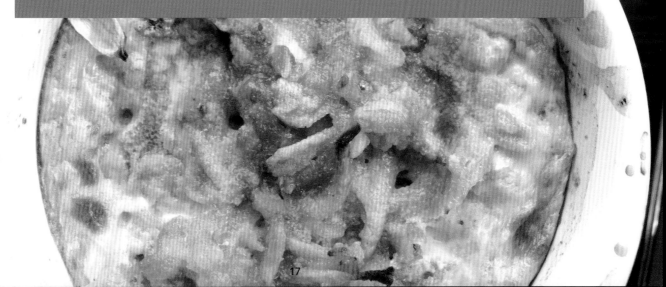

BAKED PORRIDGE BRÛLÉE
WITH APPLE & CARDAMON

This is a great recipe for days when you have more time. Baking oats gives them a lovely cake-like texture and the caramelised brown sugar substitute feels like such a treat.

SERVES 1
5 MINS PREP
35 MINS BAKE

INGREDIENTS

45g/½ cup porridge oats

100ml/½ cup milk

1 tbsp high protein yoghurt

1 small apple, grated

seeds of 5 cardamom pods

2 heaped tsp brown sugar substitute

265 CALORIES **8g** PROTEIN **4g** FAT **44g** CARBS

MACROS

METHOD

1. Preheat oven to 180°C/350°F.

2. Mix together oats, milk, yoghurt, grated apple, cardamom seeds and half of the brown sugar substitute.

3. Spoon mixture into an oven-safe ramekin and sprinkle with remaining brown sugar substitute.

4. Bake for around 35 minutes, or until browned.

FOUR BREAKFASTS
READY IN 4 MINUTES OR LESS

You know those days when you wake up in the morning with only a few minutes to spare before leaving the house? It's all too easy to pick up a croissant or sugary breakfast bar on the way to work. But here are four better options.

PROTEIN SHAKE

Surely the quickest, easiest breakfast in the world. In a protein shaker, simply **add a scoop of protein powder, a scoop of fine oats** and your choice of milk or water. Give it a good shake and drink it on your way out.

The fine oats are a good dose of slow-releasing energy to keep you going until lunchtime, but for a low carb option leave them out.

MACROS (including fine oats + water)

MICROWAVE SCRAMBLED EGGS

Scrambling your eggs in the microwave means less washing up.

Crack **a whole egg and 2 egg whites** into a mug. Season with salt & pepper and whisk with a fork. Microwave on high for 45 seconds. Add in a little **cooked meat** (e.g. ham, bacon, chorizo), stir and microwave for another 30 – 45 seconds.

MACROS (including 2 rashers of pancetta)

OATS IN A HURRY

Just like overnight oats, but without the overnight part.

Sweeten **a scoop of oats** with a little **zero calorie syrup.** Mix well and top with a **heaped tablespoon of high protein yoghurt** and whatever fruit or nuts you have in the kitchen.

MACROS (including ½ cup of grapes as shown in the picture)

FRIED EGG WITH AVOCADO ON A THIN BAGEL

My choice of a speedy breakfast. Spray a little oil into a frying pan on medium heat and crack in **an egg**. While the egg is cooking, put a **thin bagel** into the toaster and slice **half an avocado**. By the time the toaster pops up, the egg should be done.

MACROS (with everything listed)

EGGS

High in protein, versatile and inexpensive – even free range ones.
Eggs are amazing little things.

Whole egg or egg white?

Many people think of the white as the healthy part of the egg, and it's easy to see why – it has more than half the protein and zero fat.

Egg whites are now widely available in cartons, a convenient option for making omelettes.

But don't knock the yolk – it contains loads of important vitamins that you will miss out on if you throw it away. Plus, the yolk is the tasty part.

Isn't it bad to eat too many eggs?

This idea is a throwback to the days when cholesterol and saturated fat were seen as big diet no-nos. Current opinion has changed. Eggs are considered fine once again, but as with any single food, there's no need to overdo it.

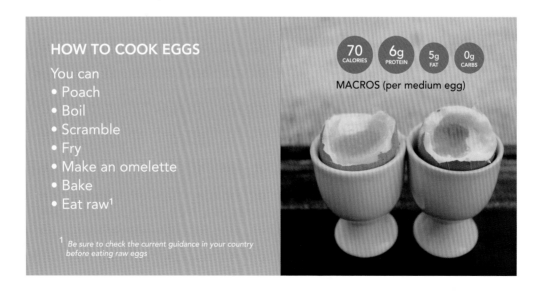

HOW TO COOK EGGS

You can
- Poach
- Boil
- Scramble
- Fry
- Make an omelette
- Bake
- Eat raw[1]

[1] *Be sure to check the current guidance in your country before eating raw eggs*

70 CALORIES   **6g** PROTEIN   **5g** FAT   **0g** CARBS

MACROS (per medium egg)

POACHED EGGS

Poaching may not be the easiest or quickest way to cook eggs, but a perfectly poached egg can't be beat.

Here is my failproof method for perfectly poached eggs every time.

SERVES 2
5 MINS PREP
5 MINS COOK

INGREDIENTS
2 eggs
a splash of white wine vinegar
salt

METHOD

1. Fill a medium-sized saucepan with cold water. Add a splash of vinegar and a pinch of salt. Bring to the boil.

2. Crack the eggs into individual cups or ramekins.

3. Once the water is bubbling steadily, turn the heat down so the water is at a gentle simmer. Using a spoon, create a gentle whirlpool in the pan, which will help the egg whites wrap around the yolks.

4. Using your other hand, gently pour in each egg.

5. Set a timer for 3 - 4 minutes, depending on how firm you want the yolks to be.

6. Using a slotted spoon, remove each egg and pat dry with kitchen paper.

HIGH PROTEIN EGGS BENEDICT

Is there anyone who doesn't drool at the thought of hollandaise sauce? This is an amazing high protein/low fat recipe from my friend, Willy Wong, and it tastes incredible.

SERVES 2
5 MINS PREP
5 MINS COOK

INGREDIENTS

100g/⅓ cup high protein yoghurt

1 tsp mustard

1 tsp white wine vinegar

a squeeze of lemon juice

2 tbsp butter

2 egg yolks

to serve
  2 poached eggs (see previous page for method)

METHOD

1. Mix together the yoghurt, mustard, vinegar and lemon juice in a bowl and set aside.
2. Melt the butter in a saucepan. Once melted, turn the heat down as low as possible and add the yoghurt mixture. Slowly whisk in the yolks and turn the heat off. If you need to reheat the sauce before serving, do it slowly to avoid curdling.
3. To serve, pour the sauce over the poached eggs.

> ### RECIPE NOTES
>
> • *This recipe is genius ... the traditional recipe for hollandaise sauce has copious amounts of butter, some of which Willy replaced with high protein yoghurt. The result is still as delicious and luxurious, but has more protein and much less fat.*

220 CALORIES | 15g PROTEIN | 16g FAT | 3g CARBS

MACROS (1 poached egg + 1 serving of hollandaise sauce)

POACHED EGGS WITH BAKED CHICKPEAS

This fantastic alternative to sugary baked beans was inspired by an Ottolenghi recipe a friend made for me. While Ottolenghi slow cooks his dried chickpeas for 5 hours, this recipe uses tinned chickpeas and is on the table in only 30 minutes.

SERVES 2
10 MINS PREP
25 MINS COOK

INGREDIENTS

400g/14oz tin chickpeas, drained

1 tsp olive oil

1 medium onion, sliced

3 garlic cloves, sliced

2 tbsp tomato puree

½ tsp chilli powder

½ tsp smoked paprika

salt & pepper

½ tsp sugar/sweetener

3 tbsp water

to serve

2 poached eggs (see page 21 for method)

METHOD

1. Heat the oil in a saucepan on low heat and fry the sliced onions and garlic for around 15 minutes. Don't rush this step, we are 'caramelizing' the onions and garlic to create flavour for a tastier finished dish.

2. Add the tomato puree, chilli powder and smoked paprika and fry for around 2 – 3 minutes, stirring constantly.

3. Let the mixture cool a little before transferring to a food processor. Season with salt & pepper, add the sugar/sweetener and blend into a paste.

4. Pour the mixture back into the pan and add the chickpeas and water. Simmer for around 5 minutes until the chickpeas are warm, adding more water if necessary.

RECIPE NOTES

- *This dish will keep for a few days in the fridge. I highly recommend making a big batch, as it will taste even better the next day when the chickpeas have absorbed the flavours.*

290 CALORIES 16g PROTEIN 12g FAT 30g CARBS

MACROS (1 poached egg + 1 serving of chickpeas)

POACHED EGG WITH COURGETTE, CARROT & FETA FRITTERS

These fritters, a creation of my friend Willy Wong, are a fantastic make-ahead breakfast (or lunch/dinner for that matter).

MAKES 10 FRITTERS
10 - 15 MINS PREP
6 MINS COOK

INGREDIENTS

250g/9oz courgettes, grated

100g/3½oz carrots, grated

50g/⅓ cup self-raising flour

25g/¼ cup/1 scoop unflavoured whey protein powder

70g/½ cup feta cheese, crumbled

1 egg

salt & pepper

1 tbsp oil

to serve
  2 poached eggs

METHOD

1. Put the grated courgettes and carrots onto a clean tea towel. Bunch the cloth up and squeeze as much liquid out as possible.

2. Add the grated vegetables to a mixing bowl with the flour, protein powder, crumbled feta cheese and egg. Mix well and season with salt & pepper. Shape the mixture into 10 small fritters.

3. Heat the oil in a large frying pan over medium heat. Add the fritters to the pan and fry for around 2 – 3 minutes, until browned. Turn and fry the other side for another 2 – 3 minutes, until cooked through.

RECIPE NOTES

- Although it's surprisingly quick to grate a carrot and a couple of courgettes, the easier option would be to buy spiralised courgette and carrot from the supermarket.

- The protein powder is optional but gives the fritters a nice extra protein boost.

380 CALORIES 24g PROTEIN 15g FAT 8g CARBS

MACROS (1 poached egg + 4 fritters)

BOILED EGGS

You know the saying 'can't even boil an egg'? That was me once. The struggle is real – getting a boiled egg exactly how you want it can be tough. The key is to wait until the water is bubbling and to keep it at a steady simmer. Below is a handy guide to timing.

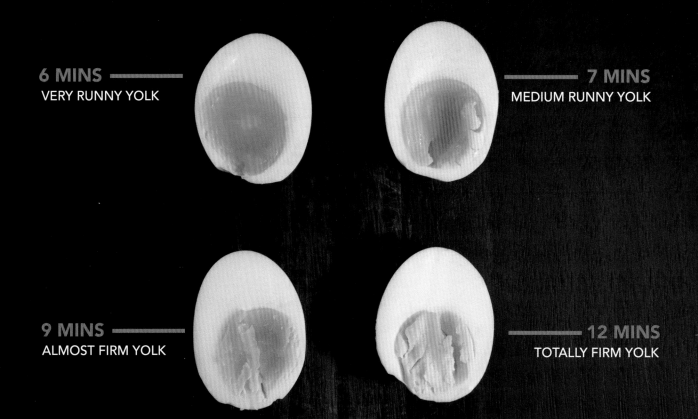

6 MINS
VERY RUNNY YOLK

7 MINS
MEDIUM RUNNY YOLK

9 MINS
ALMOST FIRM YOLK

12 MINS
TOTALLY FIRM YOLK

BOILED EGGS WITH SWEET POTATO HASH BROWNS

Here's a high protein, lower fat version of the American breakfast classic.

SERVES 2
10 MINS PREP
7 MINS COOK

INGREDIENTS

100g sweet potato, grated

40g high protein cheese[1]

1 egg

1 spring onion, chopped

salt & pepper

1 tbsp oil

to serve
4 boiled eggs,
cooked to your liking

METHOD

1. Mix together the grated sweet potato, cheese, egg, spring onion and a little salt & pepper.

2. Warm the oil in a large frying pan over a low heat and spoon in the mixture, making 4 circles. If your pan isn't big enough, you can cook the hash browns in two batches.

3. Gently fry for 3 – 4 minutes until browned before turning over and frying the second side for another 2 – 3 minutes. Once browned, remove from the pan and serve.

1 For details of where to find this, go to highproteincook.com/breakfast

| 335 CALORIES | 23g PROTEIN | 13g FAT | 12g CARBS |

MACROS (2 boiled eggs + 2 hash browns)

GROWN-UP EGG & SOLDIERS

These bring back childhood memories of dippy eggs with soldiers made from buttered toast, crusts lovingly removed.

Here are some tasty lower carb options for dipping:

1. Asparagus wrapped in streaky bacon

2. Grilled halloumi cheese

3. Asparagus wrapped in turkey bacon

4. Butternut squash cut into crinkle chips

5. Asparagus wrapped in Parma ham

FRIED EGGS

Fried eggs are extremely versatile – I put them on top of everything from salads to pizzas.

If you want a foolproof way to make perfect fried eggs, get yourself a little one-egg frying pan.[1]

PROTEIN PIZZA BASE RECIPE

MAKES 4 MINI PIZZAS

INGREDIENTS

25g/¼ cup/1 scoop pea protein powder

50g/⅓ cup self-raising flour (plus extra for dusting)

30g/¼ cup ground almonds

75g/⅓ cup high protein yoghurt

1 egg white

a tiny pinch sugar/sweetener

salt & pepper

2 tsp oil

FRIED EGG OPTIONS

1. Serve on avocado toast with samphire

2. For a colourful breakfast, serve with streaky bacon, broccoli, tomatoes and mushrooms

3. On top of breakfast protein pizza with avocado and pine nuts – recipe opposite

4. Serve with streaky bacon, mushrooms, roasted butternut squash and rocket

5. On top of quinoa mixed with roasted vegetables

6. For a huge healthy fry-up, serve with chicken sausages, Sriracha, avocado, mushrooms and broccoli

7. A perfect accompaniment to pork sausages, spinach and Sriracha

8. On a thin bagel with smoked mackerel pâté

9. Serve with turkey sausages and spinach

METHOD

1. Mix all of the ingredients except the oil into a dough. Sprinkle flour on your hands, a rolling pin and over a large, clean surface.

2. Separate the dough into 4 balls. Using the rolling pin, roll each ball into a round pizza base.

2. Heat 1 tsp of oil in a large frying pan over medium heat. When hot, carefully add two pizza bases. Cook for around 2 – 3 minutes until browned before flipping over with a spatula and cooking another 1 – 2 minutes until done.

3. Remove the pizzas and repeat step 2 for the remaining pizzas.

150 CALORIES 10g PROTEIN 5g FAT 11g CARBS

MACROS (per mini pizza base)

[1] For details of where to find this, go to highproteincook.com/breakfast

SCRAMBLED EGGS

I used to be notoriously bad at making scrambled eggs. I would use too large a pan over too high a heat and cook the eggs until they were barely edible. Luckily things have changed. Here's how I now make delicious, velvety scrambled eggs.

BASIC RECIPE

SERVES 2
5 MINS PREP
5 MINS COOK

INGREDIENTS

4 eggs, beaten
1 tsp butter or oil
salt & pepper

METHOD

1. Crack eggs into a bowl and season with a good sprinkling of salt & pepper. Whisk the eggs until they are a uniformly yellow colour.
2. Warm the butter/oil in a small saucepan over low heat. Once melted, pour in the beaten eggs.
3. Stir slowly, using a wooden spoon or spatula, bringing the eggs away from the edges of the pan.
4. Take the eggs out of the pan when they are still slightly underdone as they will continue to cook.

SCRAMBLED EGG OPTIONS

1. Mexican style scrambled eggs with chopped avocado, spring onions, coriander and hot sauce
2. On flatbread with mashed avocado and Sriracha sauce
3. With leftover chopped bacon on rye bread
4. With biltong, spinach, mushrooms and avocado
5. Masala scrambled eggs – see recipe below
6. Chinese-style scrambled eggs with tomato and a little soy sauce

MASALA SCRAMBLED EGGS

At step 2 of the basic recipe, add **a chopped small green chilli pepper** and **a small chopped red onion** to the oil or melted butter. Fry gently for around 5 minutes before adding **2 chopped tomatoes**. Cook for a further 5 minutes before adding **¼ tsp cayenne pepper**, **½ tsp turmeric powder** and the beaten eggs.

160 CALORIES | 12g PROTEIN | 12g FAT | 0g CARBS

MACROS (per serving)

OMELETTE

The key to a successful omelette is having the right-sized non-stick pan – a 24cm/9½-inch pan is perfect for a 3-egg/1 egg + 3 white omelette.

FILLING OPTIONS

1. Biltong, green chilli and cheddar cheese

2. Quinoa mixed with peppers, avocado, pomegranate, pine nuts and feta cheese

3. Chorizo, spinach and red pepper purée

4. Basic omelette with Sriracha sauce

5. Pork and apple sausage, mushrooms, broccoli and tomatoes

6. Parma ham and broccoli

7. Mushroom and goat cheese

8. Banana, raspberry, flaked almonds and zero-calorie caramel sauce

9. King prawn, asparagus and coriander

BASIC RECIPE

SERVES 1
5 MINS PREP
10 MINS COOK

INGREDIENTS

1 whole egg + 3 egg whites

salt & pepper

1 tsp oil

filling of your choice – see opposite

METHOD

1. Whisk together the eggs in a bowl using a fork, adding a good pinch of salt & pepper.

2. Heat the oil in a pan over medium heat. Once warm, pour in the beaten eggs. Roll the pan from side to side to make sure the eggs cover the base of the pan entirely.

3. Using a wooden spatula or spoon, bring the eggs away from the edges of the pan towards the centre. Then, lift up the pan a little and roll it from side to side to fill in the gap with more egg mixture.

4. Repeat step 3 until no runny parts of the egg mixture remain.

5. Add the filling ingredients over half of the omelette and using the wooden spatula, fold the other half of the omelette over the filling.

6. Cook for around 1 – 2 minutes and serve.

170 CALORIES 15g PROTEIN 10g FAT 1g CARBS

MACROS (basic recipe)

SPANISH TORTILLA

Extremely popular in Spain, these omelettes are usually made with white potato. This low-carb version tastes great cold and will keep for a couple of days in the fridge, making it perfect for a quick breakfast.

MAKES 4 SLICES
5 MINS PREP
35 MINS COOK

INGREDIENTS

1 tsp oil

½ red onion, peeled and thinly sliced

100g/3½oz butternut squash 'lasagne' sheets

2 eggs

4 egg whites

salt & pepper

METHOD

1. Heat the oil in a pan over medium heat. Once warm, add the onion and gently fry for around 10 minutes, until softened.

2. Tear the butternut squash slices into smallish pieces and add to the pan. Fry for 2 - 3 minutes.

3. Add the eggs into a mixing bowl, season with a pinch of salt & pepper and then whisk together with a fork.

4. Take the onions and butternut squash out of the pan and mix with the eggs. Put the mixture back into the pan, cover and cook over low heat for around 20 minutes, or until there is no runny egg remaining on top.

5. The easiest way to get the tortilla out of the pan is by using a plate: loosen the sides of the tortilla with a wooden spatula, place a plate over the top and being careful not to burn your hands, flip the pan over turning the omelette onto the plate.

6. Cut into wedges and serve.

RECIPE NOTES

- For this recipe, I used pre-cut butternut squash 'lasagne' sheets. If you can't get these, make thin slices yourself using a vegetable peeler. Or use larger slices and cook them for a little longer at step 2.

- This is a very basic recipe low enough in calories to justify adding all sorts of delights like cooked chorizo and bacon. Chop up and fry until crispy and then add to the egg mixture at step 4.

80 CALORIES — 7g PROTEIN — 4g FAT — 3g CARBS

MACROS (per slice)

SOUFFLÉ OMELETTE

Transform a basic omelette into a luxurious cheese soufflé with this fantastic recipe by Willy Wong. The fluffy texture of the omelette combined with the rich flavour of the Parma ham and Parmesan cheese make this dish a real treat.

SERVES 1
10 MINS PREP
10 MINS COOK

INGREDIENTS

1 egg, separated

2 egg whites

50g/⅔ cup mushrooms, finely chopped

1 tsp butter

5 asparagus spears

1 tsp Parmesan cheese

salt & pepper

2 slices of Parma ham

METHOD

1. Fry the mushrooms in a pan over low heat with ½ tsp butter for around 3 minutes, until browned. Blanch the asparagus in boiling water for around 1 minute.

2. Using an electric whisk, beat the egg whites until stiff peaks form.

3. In a separate bowl, mix together the egg yolk, Parmesan cheese and a good sprinkling of salt & pepper. Gently fold this mixture into the egg whites, being careful not to flatten the air out of them too much.

4. Reheat the frying pan over low heat and add the remaining ½ tsp butter. Once warmed, pour in the egg mixture and spread it evenly around the pan.

5. Allow the omelette to cook for around 2 – 3 minutes and then lay the asparagus, mushrooms and Parma ham over the top.

6. Place the pan under a hot grill on high for around 4 minutes, until slightly browned on top.

RECIPE NOTES

• For this recipe to work, the egg whites really do need to be whisked into stiff peaks using an electric mixer – a fork or metal whisk simply won't do the job.

• A good tip for making butter stretch further is to rub it onto the frying pan rather than melting it.

235 CALORIES 23g PROTEIN 14g FAT 2g CARBS

MACROS

BAKED EGGS 3 WAYS

The recipe name is a little deceptive as it's actually easier to make them on the hob where you can cook the yolks to your liking.

Whichever way you choose to cook them, baked eggs are perfect for a weekend brunch.

1.HUEVOS RANCHEROS

Cut **½ a corn tortilla** into strips and toast in a warm frying pan without oil. Scatter these strips over the top and add **½ a sliced avocado**.
(per serving – 305 calories, 14g protein, 19g fat, 19g carbs)

2. SHAKSHUKA

At step 3, crumble in **80g/½ cup feta cheese**. Before serving, sprinkle with chopped **coriander leaves**.
(per serving – 305 calories, 17g protein, 21g fat, 12g carbs)

3. BAKED EGGS WITH AUBERGINE AND CHICKPEAS

At step 1, add another **1 tsp oil** and ½ a sliced aubergine to the pan with the garlic and peppers. At step 3, add **½ can drained chickpeas**.
(per serving – 300 calories, 16g protein, 17g fat, 24g carbs)

BASIC RECIPE

SERVES 3
10 MINS PREP
25 MINS COOK

INGREDIENTS

5 eggs
1 tbsp olive oil
1 large onion, sliced
3 cloves of garlic, sliced
1 red pepper, deseeded and sliced
1 tsp cumin
1 tsp paprika
½ tsp cayenne pepper
salt & pepper
400g/14oz can chopped tomatoes

METHOD

1. Heat the oil in a pan over medium heat. Add the onion and gently fry for around 4 – 5 minutes, until it begins to soften. At this point, add the garlic and pepper and fry for another 4 – 5 minutes, until the onion has completely lost its crunch.

2. Stir in the cumin, paprika, cayenne pepper and salt & pepper. Add the can of tomatoes and allow the sauce to thicken for around 2 – 3 minutes.

3. Make 5 gaps in the sauce and gently break in the eggs. Put the lid on and leave for around 5 – 10 minutes, until the eggs are cooked to your liking.

4. Divide into three using a large spoon and serve.

 225 CALORIES **12g** PROTEIN **14g** FAT **12g** CARBS

MACROS (basic recipe, per serving)

1.

2.

3.

EGG MUFFINS

These are a creation of my good friend, Willy Wong. They are like mini frittatas – perfect for cooking in advance and storing for a couple of days in the fridge. All you need is a muffin tin, either silicon or well greased.

BASIC RECIPE

MAKES 6 MUFFINS
5 MINS PREP
25 MINS COOK

INGREDIENTS

3 eggs

1 tbsp milk

1 tsp baking powder

salt & pepper

extra ingredients of your choosing – see opposite for ideas

METHOD

1. Preheat oven to 180°C/350°F.
2. Whisk eggs, milk, baking powder and plenty of salt & pepper together.
3. Divide the extra ingredients between the 6 muffin tin segments and pour in the egg mixture, dividing it evenly.
4. Bake for around 25 minutes or until browned.

FETA & CHERRY TOMATO

40g/¼ cup feta cheese, 2 sliced cherry tomatoes, 2 sliced black olives and a **sprinkling of oregano**
(per muffin - 60 calories, 4g protein, 4g fat, 1g carbs)

ENGLISH BREAKFAST

A slice of lean bacon (cooked and chopped), **a lean pork sausage** (cooked and chopped), **2 small mushrooms** (chopped) and **6 tbsp baked beans**
(per muffin - 90 calories, 8g protein, 5g fat, 3g carbs)

SUN-DRIED TOMATO, SPINACH & MOZZARELLA

2 small pieces of sun-dried **tomatoes** (chopped), **20g/3 tbsp grated mozzarella cheese**, a few torn **spinach leaves** and a sprinkling of **oregano**
(per muffin - 60 calories, 5g protein, 4g fat, 0g carbs)

SEAFOOD

4 chopped seafood sticks, 40g/¼ cup cheddar and **1 chopped spring onion**
(per muffin - 65 calories, 5g protein, 3g fat, 2g carbs)

 40 CALORIES **3g** PROTEIN **3g** FAT **0g** CARBS

MACROS (per basic muffin)

BACON & EGG BREAKFAST CUPS

Easy to make and incredibly cute, these breakfast cups can be customised with whatever you want – add bread to the base, top with cheese and chives – the options are endless.

BASIC RECIPE

MAKES 6
2 MINS PREP
30 MINS COOK

INGREDIENTS
6 rashers streaky bacon
6 eggs

METHOD

1. Preheat oven to 180°C/350°F.
2. Fry the bacon rashers in a large frying pan until they are just cooked, i.e. not too crispy. Remove from the pan and let cool.
3. Using a greased muffin tin, lay each bacon rasher around the edge of each segment and break an egg into the centre.
4. Bake for around 20 – 25 minutes, until the egg whites are just set.

85 CALORIES   **5g** PROTEIN   **4g** FAT   **0g** CARBS

MACROS (per cup)

RECIPE NOTES

- *These breakfast cups are best eaten immediately, but they will keep for a few days in the fridge.*

SCOTCH EGGS

This was one of the most popular recipes of my book High Protein Classics, where I used chicken sausages. I've kept this recipe deliberately basic so you can use your imagination and adapt as you please.

BASIC RECIPE

SERVES 1
2 MINS PREP
30 MINS COOK

INGREDIENTS

1 egg
3 sausages (total weight = 170g)
1 tbsp polenta
salt & pepper

RECIPE NOTES

- Polenta is my shortcut of coating everything from chicken breasts to Scotch eggs. Panko breadcrumbs have a similar number of calories but first you need to dip the Scotch egg in two extra bowls – one with a beaten egg and one with flour – to get the breadcrumbs to stick.

- If the sausagemeat won't stick together, add a little beaten egg or egg white. If it's too sticky, add some flour or protein powder to make it more manageable.

METHOD

1. Preheat oven to 180°C/350°F.
2. Bring a saucepan of water to the boil. Add in the egg.
3. Set a timer for around 6 minutes. Remove the egg and plunge it into a bowl of cold water to stop the cooking.
4. Spread out a sheet of cling film on a chopping board and squeeze out the filling from the sausages over it. Spread the meat thinly.
5. Carefully peel the egg and place it on top of the flattened sausagemeat. Bunch up the cling film around the egg and carefully massage the sausagemeat around it so that the egg is fully covered.
6. Pour the polenta into a bowl and add a good sprinkling of salt & pepper. Remove the cling film from the Scotch egg and roll it in the polenta, coating all sides.
7. Put the Scotch egg in a baking tray and bake for around 20 minutes for a soft yolk or 25 minutes for a firmer yolk. Be sure the sausagement is cooked through before serving.

VARIATIONS:

1. Mix a little cooked bacon or chorizo into the sausagemeat
2. Use chicken, turkey or beef sausages instead of regular pork sausages

305 CALORIES   **21g** PROTEIN   **21g** FAT   **4g** CARBS

MACROS (per Scotch egg)

DAIRY

Thick dairy products are a fantastic source of casein, a slow-digesting protein. This makes them a great choice at breakfast time for helping you feel satisfied until lunchtime.

HIGH PROTEIN YOGHURT ——
(e.g. Greek, skyr)
11g of protein per 100g

QUARK ——
12g of protein per 100g

COTTAGE CHEESE ——
up to 12g of protein per 100g

SMOKED MACKEREL PÂTÉ

Oily fish is a great source of omega-3 fatty acids.

SERVES 4
10 MINS PREP

INGREDIENTS

3 smoked mackerel fillets
100g/½ cup low fat cottage cheese
2 tbsp half fat crème fraîche
1 tsp mustard
juice of ½ a lemon
freshly ground black pepper

to serve
  fresh dill
  rice cakes

METHOD

Remove the skin from the mackerel and add the fillets to a blender or food processor along with the rest of the ingredients. Mix until smooth and serve.

RECIPE NOTES

- *This pate can also be made with salmon (smoked or unsmoked) or with any other oily fish.*
- *As crème fraîche isn't exactly the kind of ingredient you are likely to have lying around in your fridge, I almost left it out of the recipe. It's completely optional but gives the finished pate a lovely creaminess.*

 230 CALORIES **17g** PROTEIN **17g** FAT **2g** CARBS

MACROS (without rice cakes)

YOGHURT 4 WAYS

Like other thick dairy products, yoghurt can be a great source of protein. There are now lots of different high protein yoghurts available: Greek yoghurt and Icelandic skyr are two great choices. Check the label – there should be around 11g of protein per 100g of yoghurt.

WHAT TO EAT WITH YOGHURT

1. Nut butter pairs beautifully with both yoghurt and banana. Sprinkle a little desiccated coconut on top for extra sweetness.

2. Ripe bananas are a fantastic natural way to sweeten yoghurt. Here's a colourful breakfast of blueberries, pomegranate seeds, banana and ground flaxseed.

3. To eat on the go: Add some yoghurt to a jar with a lid and top with grapes and mixed nuts. For extra sweetness, add some zero-calorie or maple syrup.

4. For those days when you are out of fruit, simply stir in some sugar-free jam.

MINI UPSIDE-DOWN PROTEIN CHEESECAKE

Cake for breakfast?! When the macros are as good as for this one, why not? Pack some in a box and eat it on public transport – the looks you will get from other commuters will be priceless.

MAKES 2
10 MINS PREP
30 MINS COOK
1 HOUR CHILL

INGREDIENTS

250g/1 cups high protein yoghurt

125g/⅔ cups vanilla quark

2 tbsp/½ scoop vanilla whey protein powder

1 egg

75g/½ cup blueberries

1 tsp sugar/sweetener

topping
  40g low-sugar granola
  extra blueberries

METHOD

1. Preheat oven to 160°C/320°F.
2. Mix together the yoghurt, vanilla quark, vanilla whey, egg, blueberries and sugar/sweetener in a food processor until smooth.
3. Divide this mixture between two mini springform tins.[1]
4. Bake for around 30 minutes, until the top of the cheesecake starts to become solid.
5. Remove the cheesecakes from the oven and leave them to cool a little.
6. Chill in the fridge for at least 1 hour. To serve, carefully remove the mini cheesecakes from their tins and add some granola and a few blueberries to the top of each.

RECIPE NOTES

- *If you can't get hold of vanilla quark, just use regular quark and add an extra teaspoon of sugar/ sweetener. Both fresh and frozen blueberries will work.*
- *Take the cheesecakes out of the oven as soon as the top surface becomes solid with very little wobble. It's best to err on the side of caution and undercook them a little rather than risk overcooking them.*
- *My book High Protein Sweet Treats has a full-size version of this cheesecake. I encourage you to experiment with different toppings – any kind of fruit will work or even a drizzle of melted chocolate.*

330 CALORIES   32g PROTEIN   9g FAT   27g CARBS

MACROS (per mini cheesecake)

[1] For details of where to find these, go to highproteincook.com/breakfast

COTTAGE CHEESE JELLY MOUSSE

Quick and easy to make, these little jars of mousse are perfect to eat with your breakfast or as a mid-morning snack.

MAKES 4
10 MINS PREP
2-3 HOURS CHILL

INGREDIENTS

300g/1⅓ cups low fat cottage cheese

1 sachet sugar-free jelly powder

250ml/1 cup boiling water

METHOD

1. Dissolve the jelly powder in the boiling water and stir until dissolved. Cool slightly.

2. In a blender or food processor, mix the dissolved jelly with the cottage cheese until smooth.

3. Transfer the mixture into four jars or glasses and chill for 2 – 3 hours.

RECIPE NOTES

- *These jellies can be prepared ahead and are a real treat any time of day.*

- *The recipe also works great with quark or Greek yoghurt.*

- *Although the macros are based on low fat cottage cheese, you can also use the full fat version for a creamier taste.*

60 CALORIES **8g** PROTEIN **1g** FAT **3g** CARBS

MACROS (per jelly)

PROTEIN SMOOTHIES

Jazz up your protein shake with one of these colourful options. Simply mix all of the ingredients together until smooth using a good-quality blender and serve right away.

KIWI PUMPKIN SEED

Pumpkin seed protein powder doesn't have the bitter aftertaste that many plant protein powders have, making it perfect for smoothies.

    1 kiwi fruit, peeled
    25g/¼ cup/1 scoop pumpkin seed protein powder [1]
    a few spinach leaves
    1 small ripe banana, frozen
    1 cup diluted no-added-sugar apple cordial

250 CALORIES | 18g PROTEIN | 5g FAT | 36g CARBS

MACROS

BERRY FROZEN YOGHURT

No whey protein in your cupboards? No problem – this smoothie gives you 12g of protein without it.

    ½ cup/about 30 frozen mixed berries
    100g/½ cup vanilla high protein yoghurt
    3 tbsp milk

115 CALORIES | 12g PROTEIN | 1g FAT | 11g CARBS

MACROS

ICED MOCHA

Perfect for giving you a pre-workout buzz or to help you get going in the morning.

    1 shot of espresso
    25g/¼ cup/1 scoop chocolate whey protein powder
    25ml/2 tbsp milk
    4 ice cubes

105 CALORIES | 21g PROTEIN | 2g FAT | 1g CARBS

MACROS

STRAWBERRY ICE CREAM

The name says it all – this shake tastes like strawberry ice cream.

    ½ cup/about 5 frozen strawberries
    100g/½ cup low fat cottage cheese
    1 tbsp sugar/sweetener
    3 tbsp milk

115 CALORIES | 13g PROTEIN | 2g FAT | 10g CARBS

MACROS

[1] For details of where to find this, go to highproteincook.com/breakfast

LOW CARB

While some of us love to start the day with a bowl of energising oats, others find breakfast an ideal time to keep carbs low. Here are a few tasty low carb options – be sure to also take a look at the *Eggs* section (pages 20 – 47) for many more ideas.

PIGS IN BLANKETS

Or should it be 'chicken in blankets'?

For a lower fat version of the Christmas favourite, wrap small chicken sausages in thin pancetta rashers. Roast in a 180°C/350°F oven for around 30 minutes, until golden (65 calories, 8g protein, 3g fat, 1g carbs per sausage).

SEAFOOD & SCRAMBLED EGGS IN AVOCADO BOATS

These cute boats are a low carb, high fat Paleo dream.

SERVES 2
10 MINS PREP
5 MINS COOK

INGREDIENTS

100g/3½oz smoked salmon

4 cooked king prawns

1 large avocado

1 egg

3 egg whites

1 tsp oil

salt & pepper

METHOD

1. Slice the avocado in half and remove the stone. Use the tip of a knife to score the flesh, taking care not to pierce the skin. Using a tablespoon, scoop out the flesh and slice into cubes. Keep aside the avocado skin halves.

2. Follow the instructions on page 34 to cook the scrambled eggs, remembering to season with salt & pepper.

3. Once done, mix the eggs and avocado together and put into the avocado skins. Top with the smoked salmon and king prawns.

335 CALORIES 25g PROTEIN 20g FAT 10g CARBS

MACROS (per serving)

MINUTE STEAK WITH SCRAMBLED EGGS AND ASPARAGUS

The bodybuilder's choice of breakfast. As the name suggests, minute steak can be on the table within minutes. Also known as frying or sandwich steak, this thin cut is inexpensive but can be as tough as old leather if cooked badly.

TIPS

- If you buy minute steak from the supermarket, it probably won't have been aged for very long, which means it won't have much flavour. This means you will have to add your own – this can be a marinade (see recipe opposite) or simply season with salt & pepper.

- The pan or griddle needs to be very hot. To check, cut off a little fat from the edge of the steak and add to the pan. The fat should sizzle right away.

- If you use a wet marinade, dab as much of it off as possible using kitchen paper. The steak needs to be dry when it hits the pan; otherwise it will steam in the marinade.

- Although called 'minute' steaks, 15 – 20 seconds per side should be enough time to cook a very thin steak, assuming the pan is hot enough. Using a metal spatula, press the steak down into the pan to speed things up and get a crispy finish.

TAMARIND MARINADE

MARINATES 4 STEAKS

INGREDIENTS
2 heaped tbsp tamarind paste
2 tbsp soy sauce
1 tbsp oil
1 tbsp runny honey

METHOD

1. Combine all ingredients into a plastic sandwich bag and mix together. Add the steaks, making sure they are completely covered in the marinade.

2. Remove as much air as possible from the bag and secure tightly.

3. Marinate the steaks overnight in the fridge. When it's time to cook them, remove the steaks from the bag and, using some kitchen paper, dap any excess marinade off.

4. Heat a pan or griddle as hot as possible and grill each side until browned (see Tips).

270 CALORIES **31g** PROTEIN **13g** FAT **8g** CARBS

MACROS (1 marinated steak + 1 scrambled egg + 5 asparagus spears)

NEARLY NO CARB TINY TOADS

This lighter version of the British classic Toad In The Hole uses cloud bread in place of Yorkshire pudding.

SERVES 2
10 MINS PREP
15 MINS COOK

INGREDIENTS

4 thin chicken sausages, each sliced into 3

2 eggs (yolk & whites separated)

a pinch of salt

2 tbsp cream cheese

2 tbsp/½ scoop unflavoured whey protein powder

½ tsp baking powder

METHOD

1. Preheat the oven to 180°C/350°F.

2. Add the salt to the egg whites and, using an electric mixer, whisk until very stiff.

3. In a separate bowl, mix the egg yolks, cream cheese, whey protein and baking powder. Carefully fold this mixture into the egg whites.

4. Divide this mixture between the segments of a 12-cup muffin tin and top with the sliced sausages.

5. Bake for around 15 minutes or until browned. Check that the sausages are cooked through before serving.

RECIPE NOTES
- *Cloud bread tends to stick so be sure to use a non-stick or silicone muffin tin. If you don't have one, use plenty of hard butter or coconut oil to grease each segment first.*

 200 CALORIES **25g** PROTEIN **10g** FAT **2g** CARBS

MACROS (per serving)

MISO CHICKEN SOUP

This may seem like a wild card as a breakfast choice, but don't knock it until you try it. The Japanese often have it for breakfast and if you are suffering from a cold, this soup is heaven on earth.

SERVES 2
5 MINS PREP
5 MINS COOK

INGREDIENTS

1 tbsp good-quality miso paste

1 cooked chicken breast, shredded

500ml/2¼ cups water

½ chicken stock cube

1 tbsp ginger, grated

a few kale leaves

a few oyster mushrooms, slivered

1 tsp soy sauce

black pepper

garnish
  ½ red chilli, chopped lengthwise

METHOD

1. Bring the water to the boil in a medium saucepan and add the ½ chicken stock cube, miso paste and grated ginger. Mix everything together.

2. Add the shredded chicken, kale, mushrooms, soy sauce and a good sprinkling of black pepper. Simmer for a few minutes to warm the chicken and soften the kale and mushrooms.

3. Transfer the soup to bowls, garnish with red chilli and serve.

RECIPE NOTES

- *Typically miso soup is made with dashi, a stock made from konbu and bonito flakes. Chicken stock is a convenient alternative that works surprisingly well.*

- *This soup tastes even better with homemade chicken stock. When you roast a chicken, save the carcass and put it in a large pan along with whatever root vegetables you have in the fridge (onions, garlic, carrots and celery all work well). Leave to simmer for 1 – 2 hours, strain, and voilà – homemade chicken stock.*

- *If you buy too much fresh ginger, here's a tip: freeze any pieces you don't use (no need to peel or chop). When you need ginger for a recipe, simply peel and grate it frozen.*

130 CALORIES · 21g PROTEIN · 4g FAT · 6g CARBS

MACROS (per serving)

EASY LOW CARB KEDGEREE

Kedgeree is perfect for curing a hangover or blowing away a cold. Here, rice is replaced by cauliflower, making it low carb. A curry paste is an easy alternative to lots of different spices.

SERVES 2
10 MINS PREP
20 MINS COOK

INGREDIENTS

1 fillet (approx.150g/5⅓oz) smoked haddock

1 tsp butter

½ onion, finely chopped

2 tsp mild korma curry paste

½ red chilli, finely chopped

200g/7oz cauliflower rice or couscous

juice of ½ lemon

salt & pepper

to serve

   2 eggs, boiled, shelled and quartered

   small handful fresh parsley, chopped

METHOD

1. Put the haddock fillet in a large pan and add just enough water to cover it. Bring the water to the boil and simmer for 2 – 3 minutes. Once the haddock is cooked, drain, skin and flake it.

2. Melt the butter in a pan and fry the onion over a low heat for around 10 minutes until softened. Stir in the curry paste and red chilli and cook for a further 1 – 2 minutes.

3. Add the haddock and cauliflower rice/couscous. Season well with salt & pepper and stir over a medium heat for around 5 minutes to combine the flavours.

4. Squeeze in the lemon juice and top with the boiled egg quarters and chopped parsley.

RECIPE NOTES

- *Cauliflower rice or couscous is a fantastic low carb substitute for rice. You can buy it fresh, frozen or vacuum packed or you can make your own at home using a food processor.*

MACROS (per serving)

ALMOST FAT FREE FRY UP

Although no longer considered a diet no-no, it's important to remember that fat has over twice as many calories per gram than protein or carbs (fat contains nine calories, whereas protein and carbs contain only four). Like everything, it's all about balance – choosing lean breakfast options means you can treat yourself to some nut butter or avocado later in the day.

LEAN BREAKFAST OPTIONS

CHICKEN & TURKEY SAUSAGES

Sausages are not usually thought of as particularly healthy as they can have as much as 10 grams of fat each. Pork sausages rely on their fat content to give them their juiciness and tend to become dry when the fat is taken away.

As chicken and turkey are both naturally leaner meats, with a higher moisture content than pork, sausages made from these meats tend to be succulent despite being low fat.

While pork sausages are usually best grilled, chicken and turkey sausages keep their juiciness better if cooked in an uncovered frying pan. Use a little oil, and cook for around 10 minutes, depending on the thickness of the sausages.

EGG WHITES

Although slightly tasteless on their own, strong flavours like parsley or garlic transform egg whites into a tasty treat.

Using a fork or whisk, beat as much air as possible into egg whites to pump up the volume and make them fluffy.

TURKEY BACON

Although meat purists may wince at the name, turkey bacon is a great lean alternative to regular pork bacon. Basically it's thinly sliced turkey breast which is cured for around a month, giving it a smoky bacon-like taste.

While supermarket turkey bacon tends to be highly processed, hand-cured turkey bacon is in a different class and is worth the effort to find.[1]

[1] *For details of where to find this, go to highproteincook.com/breakfast*

VEGETARIAN/VEGAN

Getting enough protein from a plant-based diet can be a challenge. Below are a few suggestions – be sure to mix your protein sources to get all of the essential amino acids.[1]

QUINOA
6g of protein per 100g

BEANS
up to 8g of protein per 100g

HEMP
5g of protein per heaped tbsp

TOFU
7g of protein per 100g

[1] For more info on this, head to highproteincook/plantprotein

QUINOA PORRIDGE

Leftover quinoa makes a nice change from oats in your morning porridge.

SERVES 1
2 MINS PREP
2-3 MINS COOK

INGREDIENTS

140g/¾ cup cooked quinoa

50ml/¼ cup milk

plus
  extra protein
  something to sweeten
  toppings
(see pages 12 – 13 for suggestions)

METHOD

1. Put the quinoa and milk in a small saucepan over medium heat and gently warm through, around 2 – 3 minutes.

2. Pour the mixture into a bowl and add your chosen toppings.

RECIPE NOTES

• *Quinoa porridge is usually made with quinoa flakes. If you don't have any cooked quinoa, the flakes are more convenient, but they can be hard to find.[1] Vacuum-packed precooked quinoa is another option.*

[1] For details of where to find this, go to highproteincook.com/breakfast

| 265 CALORIES | 9g PROTEIN | 6g FAT | 40g CARBS |

MACROS (quinoa + milk only)

VEGGIE FRY UP

Beans are a vegan/vegetarian's secret weapon for getting enough protein. While not a complete protein, combine beans with grains (such as toast) in order to get all the essential amino acids.

SMOKY HOMEMADE BAKED BEANS WITH VEGGIE SAUSAGES

While time consuming, these beans are worth the effort – slow-cooked caramelized onions pair beautifully with smoked paprika.

SERVES 2
5 MINS PREP
30-35 MINS COOK

INGREDIENTS

400g/14oz tin haricot beans

1 tbsp oil

1 large onion, peeled and sliced

2 garlic cloves, crushed

1 tbsp balsamic vinegar

½ tsp smoked paprika

1 tbsp brown sugar substitute

2 tbsp tomato puree

100g/3½oz tin tomatoes

salt & pepper

METHOD

1. Heat the oil in a medium pan over low heat and add the onions, garlic and a good pinch of salt. Fry gently until the onions turn slightly golden, for around 15 – 20 minutes, stirring occasionally to prevent burning.

2. Stir in the balsamic vinegar, smoked paprika and brown sugar substitute and cook gently for another 5 minutes.

3. Add the tomato puree, tinned tomatoes and a good grinding of pepper. Simmer for around 5 minutes, until slightly thickened. Cool slightly.

4. Using a hand blender or food processor, mix the sauce until smooth. Return to the pan and add the beans. Simmer for around 5 minutes, until the beans are warm.

VEGETARIAN SAUSAGES

Vegetarian sausages are usually made with protein extracted from soybeans. There are lots of different brands to choose from, all of which taste completely different, so it's simply a case of finding your favourite.

235 CALORIES 10g PROTEIN 9g FAT 26g CARBS

MACROS (per serving)

SCRAMBLED TOFU

This is a fantastic vegan alternative to scrambled eggs. Tofu is low in calories yet high in protein.

SERVES 2
5 MINS PREP
11 MINS COOK

INGREDIENTS

200g/7oz/½ pack tofu

½ small red onion, chopped finely

1 tsp oil

½ tsp turmeric (optional)

1 tbsp nutritional yeast (optional)

METHOD

1. First, heat the oil in medium pan over medium heat. Add the chopped onion and fry for around 5 minutes, until softened.

2. Sprinkle in the turmeric and fry a minute longer.

3. Add the tofu in the pan and, using a potato masher or a fork, crumble it.

4. Cook another 5 minutes, sprinkle in the nutritional yeast and serve.

RECIPE NOTES

- *Tofu itself is quite bland and will take on the flavours of whatever you add to it. The options are endless – garlic, chopped chilli, herbs or even your favourite sauce. I prefer silken tofu for this recipe, but firm tofu is also an option.*

- *Turmeric is included mainly for its yellow colouring, making the dish appear more like scrambled eggs. Feel free to leave it out.*

- *A good source of vitamin B12, nutritional yeast is popular with vegans. It has an interesting flavour, which you either love or hate.[1]*

MACROS (per serving)

105 CALORIES · 8g PROTEIN · 6g FAT · 5g CARBS

[1] *For details of where to find this, go to highproteincook.com/breakfast*

PROTEIN PANCAKES 3 WAYS

Pancakes are probably the easiest thing you can make with protein powder. Remember protein powder is very dry – you need to include a 'wet' ingredient (e.g. sweet potato, yoghurt, banana) to counteract this. Otherwise you will end up with cardboard-like pancakes that even the dog will refuse to eat.

SWEET POTATO PANCAKES

Naturally sweet yet savoury, these are great served with turkey bacon.

SERVES 2
15 MINS PREP
5 MINS COOK

INGREDIENTS
1 medium sweet potato, baked
2 eggs
25g/¼ cup/1 scoop unflavoured whey protein powder
salt & pepper
1 tbsp oil

METHOD

1. Slice open the baked sweet potato and scoop the insides out into a mixing bowl. Once cooled, crack in the eggs and add the whey protein. Season with salt & pepper and mix everything together.

2. Heat the oil in a large frying pan over medium heat. Once warmed, spoon in the pancake batter to make 4 small pancakes.

3. Fry the first side for around 2 – 3 minutes, until browned. Flip and cook the other side another 1 – 2 minutes.

4. Once done, lift the pancakes out and serve.

| 255 CALORIES | 17g PROTEIN | 14g FAT | 13g CARBS |

MACROS (per serving)

YOGHURT PROTEIN PANCAKES

This is my new favourite protein pancake recipe. Milk is replaced by yoghurt, giving the pancakes a thicker, softer texture. You can use a whole egg rather than 2 egg whites if you prefer.

BASIC RECIPE

SERVES 2
5 MINS PREP
5 MINS COOK

INGREDIENTS

2 egg whites

2 tbsp coconut flour

50g/¼ cup high protein yoghurt

25g/¼ cup/1 scoop vanilla whey protein powder

½ tsp baking powder

1 tbsp oil

METHOD

1. Mix together the egg whites, coconut flour, yoghurt, vanilla whey and baking powder, making sure there are no lumps.

2. Heat the oil in a large frying pan over medium heat. Once warmed, spoon in the pancake batter to make 4 small pancakes.

3. Fry the first side for around 2 – 3 minutes, until browned. Flip and cook the other side another 1 – 2 minutes.

4. Once done, lift the pancakes out and serve.

MACROS (basic recipe, per serving)

BANANA ALMOND & OAT EGGLESS PANCAKES

I made this recipe by accident one day when I ran out of eggs. The pancakes don't stick together as well as in the other recipes, but they taste great.

SERVES 2

INGREDIENTS

1 medium ripe banana

25g/¼ cup fine oats

25g/¼ cup/1 scoop protein powder of your choice

1 tbsp almond butter

60ml/¼ cup milk

1 tbsp oil

METHOD

1. Mash the banana until smooth, and then add the oats, protein powder, milk and almond butter. Mix everything together.

2. Heat the oil in a large frying pan over medium heat. Once warmed, spoon in the pancake batter to make 6 – 8 small pancakes.

3. Fry the first side for around 2 – 3 minutes, until browned. Flip very carefully and cook the other side another 1 – 2 minutes.

4. Once both sides are browned, take out of the pan and serve.

MACROS (per serving)

ALMOND BUTTER STUFFED PANCAKES

At least 2 hours beforehand, spoon **4 teaspoons of almond butter** onto a sheet of greaseproof paper, making 4 separate circles. Freeze until solid, for 1 – 2 hours. Put half the batter in the pan to create four pancakes, place a circle of frozen almond butter on top of each pancake, pressing down a little, and cover with the remaining batter.

PANCAKES WITH BLUEBERRY SAUCE

Add ½ **cup blueberries** (fresh or frozen) to a small saucepan together with 1 tsp brown sugar substitute and 2 tbsp of water. Heat gently for 5 minutes, bursting the blueberries with a fork as they soften. Spoon this sauce over the cooked pancakes.

PROTEIN FRENCH TOAST

Why have whey protein as a boring shake when you can transform it into this delicious breakfast treat? Serve with some zero-calorie syrup or, if you are feeling indulgent, maple syrup.

MAKES 3
5 MINS PREP
5 MINS COOK

INGREDIENTS

25g/¼ cup/1 scoop vanilla whey protein powder

120ml/½ cup milk

2 eggs

3 large slices of bread

1 tbsp oil

METHOD

1. Mix together the vanilla whey, milk and eggs, making sure there are no lumps. Pour the mixture onto a large plate. Add the bread, let it soak a few minutes and turn it over so both sides become saturated.

2. Heat the oil in a large frying pan over medium heat. Once hot, add the soaked bread. You may need to do this in two batches, unless you have a huge frying pan. Fry for around 2 – 3 minutes, until the first side is browned, and then flip to cook the other side.

3. Serve with your choice of toppings.

RECIPE NOTES

- *You can use any kind of bread for this recipe (macros are based on wholemeal bread). The thicker the bread, the longer you need to cook it and over a lower heat so it doesn't burn.*

- *Coconut or any other mild oil works well for this recipe. Don't use extra-virgin olive oil – it has too strong a flavour.*

240 CALORIES · 16g PROTEIN · 11g FAT · 17g CARBS

MACROS (per serving)

LOW CARB TOAST ALTERNATIVES

PORTOBELLO MUSHROOM TOAST

1. Clean the mushrooms and remove the stems. Brush both sides with olive oil and season with salt & pepper.

2. Preheat grill to high and place the mushrooms on a grill grate without crowding. Grill, gill-side up, for around 5 minutes, before flipping and grilling the other side for another 5 minutes.

TOPPING IDEAS

A fried egg
Smoked salmon
Grilled halloumi cheese
Mashed avocado
Cooked spinach
Nut butter (a weird combo but it tastes great)